# *on a more serious note*
# OUR COPYRIGHT NOTE

G000046663

# PUSH POWER BOSS JOURNAL + PLANNER

**PUBLISHER**
**TA MEDIA & PRODUCTIONS LLC**
**DALLAS, TX 75240**
**www.PUBLISHYOURBOOKTODAY.INFO**
**WWW.TAMEDIACO.COM**

# *let's get started*
# WHAT'S INSIDE
# 01

REFLECT ON 2020 TO CELEBRATE YOUR BIG ACCOMPLISHMENTS AND LEARN FROM YOUR CHALLENGES. SET NEW 2021 INTENTIONS WITH ACTIONABLE WORKSHEETS THAT WILL GUIDE YOU TO CREATE ACHIEVABLE PLANS IN YOUR BUSINESS. PLAN OUT YOUR DAYS, WEEKS, AND ENTIRE YEAR WITH ORGANIZED PLANNERS THAT WILL HELP YOU STAY FOCUSED ON WHAT REALLY MATTERS. SET FINANCIAL GOALS TO HELP YOU GROW YOUR ABUNDANCE MINDSET IN YOUR BUSINESS.

# let's get started
## WHAT'S INSIDE
# 02

- QUOTE PAGENOTE TO SELF (FILL-IN)
- 4 MONTHLY
- WEEKLY
- DAILY INTENTION PAGES
- GRATITUDE JOURNAL PAGE2
- PAST YEAR REFLECTION JOURNAL PAGES
- LOOKING FORWARD JOURNAL PAGES
- BLANK JOURNAL PAGE
- 4 GOAL SETTING PAGES
- 3 MONTHLY, WEEKLY,
- DAILY PLANNER PAGES
- PROJECT PLANNER PAGE
- 3 FINANCIAL PLANNER
- PAGES
- HOLIDAYS
- 12 MONTHLY CALENDAR PAGES
- FILL-IN CALENDAR PAGE

*bio*

Cheronda Hester CEO of Push Power Boss. Her goal is to empower women in the areas of self-esteem, self-worth, and self-growth. By providing knowledge, direction, self-awareness through books, workshops, seminars, programs, one on one counseling, and mentorship. Developing women to add value to their present and futuristic spheres of influence. She is a true believer of Proverbs 27:17 "Iron Sharpens Iron"!

# TRUE SUCCESS IS FOUND IN SEEKING GOD WITH OUR WHOLE HEART, MIND, SOUL, AND STRENGTH!!!!

# FEAR
## HAS TWO
## MEANINGS,
### FORGET EVERYTHING
## AND RUN,
#### OR
### FACE EVERYTHING
## AND RISE,
### THE CHOICE IS YOURS.

i

can

AND

I will

*speaker, life coach, credit specialist*

# CHERONDA L. HESTER

CONNECT ACROSS ALL
SOCIAL MEDIA PLATFORMS
JOIN OUR EMAIL LIST AT
**WWW.PUSHPOWERBOSS.COM**

*#pushpowerboss*

# You Have to Believe

*quote of the year*

# FOR LAST YEAR'S WORDS BELONG TO LAST YEAR'S LANGUAGE

## AND NEXT YEAR'S WORDS AWAIT ANOTHER VOICE

*T s elliot*

# PUSH power BOSS

# NOTE TO SELF

*dear.* _____

YOU HAVE COME SO FAR THIS YEAR. LOOK AT ALL YOU'VE _____ ALREADY. NEXT YEAR YOU WILL LOOK BACK & SEE YOU WERE _____ ALL ALONG. IN A YEAR YOU'LL BE _____ & _____ . I'M SO VERY PROUD OF YOU.

*love you always,*

_____
SIGN YOUR NAME HERE

# monthly intentions

_____

### OPEN PROJECTS

_____
_____
_____
_____
_____
_____
_____
_____
_____

**I AM**

### MONTHLY INTENTIONS

01: _____

_____

02: _____

_____

03: _____

_____

04: _____

_____

05: _____

_____

06: _____

_____

07: _____

_____

A FEELING OF TOTAL PEACE

# weekly priorities

WEEK OF:

_____

| MONDAY |
| --- |
| _____ |
| _____ |
| _____ |

| TUESDAY |
| --- |
| _____ |
| _____ |
| _____ |

| WEDNESDAY |
| --- |
| _____ |
| _____ |
| _____ |

| THURSDAY |
| --- |
| _____ |
| _____ |
| _____ |

| FRIDAY |
| --- |
| _____ |
| _____ |
| _____ |

| SAT / SUN |
| --- |
| _____ |
| _____ |
| _____ |

## DAILY FOCUS

monday

tuesday

wednesday

thursday

friday

saturday

sunday

# today's intentions

TODAY'S DATE:

| TODAY'S TOP 3 INTENTIONS |
|---|
| 01: |
| 02: |
| 03: |

## let's do this

_____
_____
_____
_____
_____
_____
_____
_____
_____
_____
_____
_____
_____
_____

## today's affirmations

# I AM

DAILY WATER TRACKER

| HABIT TRACKER | | | | | | | |
|---|---|---|---|---|---|---|---|
| | M | T | W | T | F | S | S |
| | M | T | W | T | F | S | S |
| | M | T | W | T | F | S | S |

i'm not here
TO BE
*Average*

I'M HERE
TO BE
*Awesome*

# today's intentions

TODAY'S DATE:

_____

## CALLS / EMAILS

- _____
- _____
- _____
- _____
- _____
- _____
- _____

## HABIT TRACKER

## DEADLINES

_____
_____
_____
_____
_____
_____
_____

| TODAY I AM THANKFUL FOR |
| --- |
| 01: |
| 02: |
| 03: |

# today's to do

- _____
- _____
- _____
- _____
- _____
- _____
- _____

- _____
- _____
- _____
- _____
- _____
- _____
- _____

# gratitude reflection

## GRATITUDE LIST:

01:
_____

_____

02:
_____

_____

03:
_____

_____

04:
_____

_____

05:
_____

_____

06:
_____

_____

07:
_____

_____

08:
_____

_____

09:
_____

_____

10:
_____

_____

11:
_____

_____

## PEOPLE I'M THANKFUL FOR:

01:
_____

_____

02:
_____

_____

03:
_____

_____

04:
_____

_____

05:
_____

_____

### favorite memories

# past year reflections

## WHAT MOTIVATED YOU?

## YOUR BIGGEST STRUGGLE?

| TOP 3 ACCOMPLISHMENTS MADE THIS YEAR |
|---|
| O1: |
| O2: |
| O3: |

### 3 LESSONS LEARNED

01:

02:

03:

### 3 THINGS YOU CREATED

01:

02:

03:

## WHAT WILL YOU TAKE WITH YOU IN 2021 & WHAT WILL YOU LEAVE BEHIND?

# past year reflections

## DESCRIBE YOUR PAST YEAR IN ONE WORD

| BIGGEST WINS OF THE YEAR |
| --- |
| 01: |
| 02: |
| 03: |

| BIGGEST CHALLENGES |
| --- |
| 01: |
| 02: |
| 03: |

### LESSONS LEARNED FROM WINS

01:

02:

03:

### FROM CHALLENGES

01:

02:

03:

## PEOPLE WHO SUPPORTED YOU THIS YEAR:

when you are finished, be sure to let these people know what they mean to you

# GOD WILL direct My STEPS.

# looking forward

BRAINSTORM 10 WORDS THAT YOU WANT TO EMBODY 2021

| 3 SMALL MANIFESTATIONS |
| --- |
| 01: |
| 02: |
| 03: |

| 3 BIG MANIFESTATIONS |
| --- |
| 01: |
| 02: |
| 03: |

4 WAYS YOU WILL PUSH PAST YOUR COMFORT ZONE THIS YEAR

01:

02:

03:

04:

PICK ONE WORD FROM ABOVE TO EMBODY 2021

# abundance journal

5 WORDS THAT DESCRIBE CURRENT BELIEFS TOWARDS MONEY

## MONEY MANIFESTATIONS

01:

02:

03:

04:

05:

06:

07:

NEW OPPORTUNITIES TO
MANIFEST MORE ABUNDANCE

MY ABUNDANCE MINDSET
ALLOWS ME TO...

CURRENT RELATIONSHIP TO
ABUNDANCE IN MY BUSINESS

## ABUNDANCE AFFIRMATIONS

I AM

# BRILLIANT *thoughts*

# BRILLIANT *thoughts*

# BRILLIANT *thoughts*

# BRILLIANT *thoughts*

# BRILLIANT *thoughts*

# BRILLIANT *thoughts*

_____
_____
_____
_____
_____
_____
_____
_____
_____
_____
_____
_____
_____
_____
_____
_____
_____
_____
_____
_____
_____
_____
_____

# BRILLIANT *thoughts*

# BRILLIANT *thoughts*

# WEEKLY GOALS *week of*

## MONDAY GOAL

### ACTIONS STEPS

_____

_____

_____

_____

_____

_____

_____

## TUESDAY GOAL

### ACTIONS STEPS

_____

_____

_____

_____

_____

_____

_____

## WEDNESDAY GOAL

### ACTIONS STEPS

_____

_____

_____

_____

_____

_____

_____

## THURSDAY GOAL

### ACTIONS STEPS

_____

_____

_____

_____

_____

_____

## FRIDAY GOAL

### ACTIONS STEPS

_____

_____

_____

_____

_____

_____

## SAT/SUN GOAL

### ACTIONS STEPS

_____

_____

_____

_____

_____

_____

# this year's intentions

WORD OF THE YEAR:

_____

BUSINESS INTENTIONS:

ACTION STEPS:

01

02

03

04

FINANCIAL INTENTIONS:

ACTION STEPS:

01

02

03

04

GROWTH INTENTIONS:

ACTION STEPS:

01

02

03

04

# BUSINESS GOALS *today's date:*

### NEW PROJECTS:
- _____
- _____
- _____
- _____
- _____
- _____
- _____
- _____

### NEW CLIENTS:
- _____
- _____
- _____
- _____
- _____
- _____
- _____
- _____

### FINANCIAL:
- _____
- _____
- _____
- _____
- _____
- _____
- _____
- _____

### SOCIAL MEDIA:
- _____
- _____
- _____
- _____
- _____
- _____
- _____

### MARKETING:
- _____
- _____
- _____
- _____
- _____
- _____
- _____

### MINDSET:
- _____
- _____
- _____
- _____
- _____
- _____
- _____

# goal setting planner

START DATE: _____  DEADLINE: _____

## MY BRILLIANT GOAL:

## MY BIG WHY BEHIND THIS:

| GOAL ACTION STEPS: | DEADLINE: |
|---|---|
| 01: | |
| 02: | |
| 03: | |
| 04: | |
| 05: | |
| 06: | |
| 07: | |
| 08: | |
| 09: | |

# goal setting planner

START DATE: _____

DEADLINE: _____

## MY BRILLIANT GOAL:

## MY BIG WHY BEHIND THIS:

| GOAL ACTION STEPS: | DEADLINE: |
|---|---|
| 01: | |
| 02: | |
| 03: | |
| 04: | |
| 05: | |
| 06: | |
| 07: | |
| 08: | |
| 09: | |

# DAY PLANNER *today's date:*

| Time | |
|---|---|
| 7:00 | |
| 8:00 | |
| 9:00 | |
| 10:00 | |
| 11:00 | |
| 12:00 | |
| 1:00 | |
| 2:00 | |
| 3:00 | |
| 4:00 | |
| 5:00 | |
| 6:00 | |
| 7:00 | |
| 8:00 | |

# WEEKLY PLANNER

*morning*　　　*afternoon*　　　*evening*

| | morning | afternoon | evening |
|---|---|---|---|
| **MON** | | | |
| **TUE** | | | |
| **WED** | | | |
| **THU** | | | |
| **FRI** | | | |
| **SAT** | | | |
| **SUN** | | | |

# YEARLY PLANNER

*write out your goals, intentions & plans*

| JAN | FEB | MAR |
| --- | --- | --- |
|     |     |     |

| APR | MAY | JUN |
| --- | --- | --- |
|     |     |     |

| JUL | AUG | SEP |
| --- | --- | --- |
|     |     |     |

| OCT | NOV | DEC |
| --- | --- | --- |
|     |     |     |

# PROJECT PLANNER *name of project:*

|  | MON | TUE | WED | THU | FRI | SAT | SUN |
|---|---|---|---|---|---|---|---|
| **WEEK 1** | | | | | | | |
| **WEEK 2** | | | | | | | |
| **WEEK 3** | | | | | | | |
| **WEEK 4** | | | | | | | |

# PROJECT PLANNER
*name of project:*

| | MON | TUE | WED | THU | FRI | SAT | SUN |
|---|---|---|---|---|---|---|---|
| **WEEK 1** | | | | | | | |
| **WEEK 2** | | | | | | | |
| **WEEK 3** | | | | | | | |
| **WEEK 4** | | | | | | | |

# PROJECT PLANNER *name of project:*

|  | MON | TUE | WED | THU | FRI | SAT | SUN |
|---|---|---|---|---|---|---|---|
| **WEEK 1** | | | | | | | |
| **WEEK 2** | | | | | | | |
| **WEEK 3** | | | | | | | |
| **WEEK 4** | | | | | | | |

# PROJECT PLANNER
## name of project:

| | MON | TUE | WED | THU | FRI | SAT | SUN |
|---|---|---|---|---|---|---|---|
| **WEEK 1** | | | | | | | |
| **WEEK 2** | | | | | | | |
| **WEEK 3** | | | | | | | |
| **WEEK 4** | | | | | | | |

# PROJECT PLANNER *name of project:*

|  | MON | TUE | WED | THU | FRI | SAT | SUN |
|---|---|---|---|---|---|---|---|
| **WEEK 1** | | | | | | | |
| **WEEK 2** | | | | | | | |
| **WEEK 3** | | | | | | | |
| **WEEK 4** | | | | | | | |

# SALE GOALS & PROJECTIONS *month of:*

| REVENUE GOAL: | |
|---|---|
| # OF SALES NEEDED: | |

| PRODUCT SOLD | QTY | AMOUNT |
|---|---|---|
| | | |
| | | |
| | | |
| | | |
| | | |
| | | |

| SALE LOCATION (ETSY, WEBSITE) | SALES TOTAL |
|---|---|
| | |
| | |
| | |
| | |

| FINAL INCOME: | |
|---|---|
| FINAL # OF SALES: | |

# INCOME & EXPENSES *yearly overview*

| MONTH | EXPENSES | INCOME | TOTAL |
|-------|----------|--------|-------|
| JAN   |          |        |       |
| FEB   |          |        |       |
| MAR   |          |        |       |
| APR   |          |        |       |
| MAY   |          |        |       |
| JUN   |          |        |       |
| JUL   |          |        |       |
| AUG   |          |        |       |
| SEP   |          |        |       |
| OCT   |          |        |       |
| NOV   |          |        |       |
| DEC   |          |        |       |

TOTAL NET INCOME: _____

# INCOME & EXPENSES *monthly breakdown*

| INCOME GOAL: | |
|---|---|
| SAVINGS GOAL: | |

| GROSS MONTHLY INCOME | AMOUNT |
|---|---|
| | |
| | |
| | |
| | |
| | |
| | |
| | |

| BILLS & EXPENSES | AMOUNT | DUE |
|---|---|---|
| | | |
| | | |
| | | |
| | | |
| | | |
| | | |
| | | |

| TOTAL INCOME | |
|---|---|
| TOTAL EXPENSES | |
| TOTAL PROFIT/LOSS | |

# HOLIDAYS & DAYS OFF *rest and recharge*

| | | |
|---|---|---|
| **JAN 01**<br>NEW YEARS DAY | **FEB 15**<br>PRESIDENT'S DAY | **MAY 10**<br>MOTHER'S DAY |
| **SEP 06**<br>LABOR DAY | **JUNE 20**<br>FATHER'S DAY | **NOV 11**<br>VETERN'S DAY |
| **NOV 25**<br>THANKSGIVING | **JUL 04**<br>INDEPENDENCE DAY | **DEC 24**<br>CHRISTMAS EVE |
| **DEC 25**<br>CHRISTMAS DAY | **MAY 31**<br>MEMORIAL DAY | **MAR 23**<br>BIRTHDAY |

# janurary 2021

| SUN | MON | TUE | WED | THU | FRI | SAT |
|-----|-----|-----|-----|-----|-----|-----|
| 27 | 28 | 29 | 30 | 31 | 1 | 2 |
| 3 | 4 | 5 | 6 | 7 | 8 | 9 |
| 10 | 11 | 12 | 13 | 14 | 15 | 16 |
| 17 | 18 | 19 | 20 | 21 | 22 | 23 |
| 24 | 25 | 26 | 27 | 28 | 29 | 30 |
| 31 | 1 | 2 | 3 | 4 | 5 | 6 |

# february 2021

| SUN | MON | TUE | WED | THU | FRI | SAT |
|-----|-----|-----|-----|-----|-----|-----|
| 31 | 1 | 2 | 3 | 4 | 5 | 6 |
| 7 | 8 | 9 | 10 | 11 | 12 | 13 |
| 14 | 15 | 16 | 17 | 18 | 19 | 20 |
| 21 | 22 | 23 | 24 | 25 | 26 | 27 |
| 28 | 1 | 2 | 3 | 4 | 5 | 6 |
| 7 | 4 | 5 | 6 | 7 | 8 | 9 |

# march 2021

| SUN | MON | TUE | WED | THU | FRI | SAT |
|-----|-----|-----|-----|-----|-----|-----|
| 28 | 1 | 2 | 3 | 4 | 5 | 6 |
| 7 | 8 | 9 | 10 | 11 | 12 | 13 |
| 14 | 15 | 16 | 17 | 18 | 19 | 20 |
| 21 | 22 | 23 | 24 | 25 | 26 | 27 |
| 28 | 29 | 26 | 27 | 28 | 29 | 30 |
| 31 | 1 | 2 | 3 | 4 | 5 | 6 |

# april 2021

| SUN | MON | TUE | WED | THU | FRI | SAT |
|-----|-----|-----|-----|-----|-----|-----|
| 28 | 29 | 30 | 31 | 1 | 2 | 3 |
| 4 | 5 | 6 | 7 | 8 | 9 | 10 |
| 11 | 12 | 13 | 14 | 15 | 16 | 17 |
| 18 | 19 | 20 | 21 | 22 | 23 | 24 |
| 25 | 26 | 27 | 28 | 29 | 30 | 1 |
| 2 | 3 | 4 | 5 | 6 | 7 | 8 |

# may 2021

| SUN | MON | TUE | WED | THU | FRI | SAT |
|-----|-----|-----|-----|-----|-----|-----|
| 25 | 26 | 27 | 28 | 29 | 30 | 1 |
| 2 | 3 | 4 | 5 | 6 | 7 | 8 |
| 9 | 10 | 11 | 12 | 13 | 14 | 15 |
| 16 | 17 | 18 | 19 | 20 | 21 | 22 |
| 23 | 24 | 25 | 26 | 27 | 28 | 29 |
| 30 | 31 | 1 | 2 | 3 | 4 | 5 |

# june 2021

| SUN | MON | TUE | WED | THU | FRI | SAT |
|-----|-----|-----|-----|-----|-----|-----|
| 30 | 31 | 1 | 2 | 3 | 4 | 5 |
| 6 | 7 | 8 | 9 | 10 | 11 | 12 |
| 13 | 14 | 15 | 16 | 17 | 18 | 19 |
| 20 | 21 | 22 | 23 | 24 | 25 | 26 |
| 27 | 28 | 29 | 30 | 1 | 2 | 3 |
| 4 | 5 | 6 | 7 | 8 | 9 | 10 |

# july 2021

| SUN | MON | TUE | WED | THU | FRI | SAT |
|-----|-----|-----|-----|-----|-----|-----|
| 27 | 28 | 29 | 30 | 1 | 2 | 3 |
| 4 | 5 | 6 | 7 | 8 | 9 | 10 |
| 11 | 12 | 13 | 14 | 15 | 16 | 17 |
| 18 | 19 | 20 | 21 | 22 | 23 | 24 |
| 25 | 26 | 27 | 28 | 29 | 30 | 31 |
| 1 | 2 | 3 | 4 | 5 | 6 | 7 |

# august 2021

| SUN | MON | TUE | WED | THU | FRI | SAT |
|-----|-----|-----|-----|-----|-----|-----|
| 1 | 2 | 3 | 4 | 5 | 6 | 7 |
| 8 | 9 | 10 | 11 | 12 | 13 | 14 |
| 15 | 16 | 17 | 18 | 19 | 20 | 21 |
| 22 | 23 | 24 | 25 | 26 | 27 | 28 |
| 29 | 30 | 31 | 1 | 2 | 3 | 4 |
| 5 | 6 | 7 | 8 | 9 | 10 | 11 |

# september 2021

| SUN | MON | TUE | WED | THU | FRI | SAT |
|---|---|---|---|---|---|---|
| 29 | 30 | 31 | 1 | 2 | 3 | 4 |
| 5 | 6 | 7 | 8 | 9 | 10 | 11 |
| 12 | 13 | 14 | 15 | 16 | 17 | 18 |
| 19 | 20 | 21 | 22 | 23 | 24 | 25 |
| 26 | 27 | 28 | 29 | 30 | 1 | 2 |
| 3 | 4 | 5 | 6 | 7 | 8 | 9 |

# october 2021

| SUN | MON | TUE | WED | THU | FRI | SAT |
|---|---|---|---|---|---|---|
| 26 | 27 | 28 | 29 | 30 | 1 | 2 |
| 3 | 4 | 5 | 6 | 7 | 8 | 9 |
| 10 | 11 | 12 | 13 | 14 | 15 | 16 |
| 17 | 18 | 19 | 20 | 21 | 22 | 23 |
| 24 | 25 | 26 | 27 | 28 | 29 | 30 |
| 31 | 1 | 2 | 3 | 4 | 5 | 6 |

# november 2021

| SUN | MON | TUE | WED | THU | FRI | SAT |
|---|---|---|---|---|---|---|
| 31 | 1 | 2 | 3 | 4 | 5 | 6 |
| 7 | 8 | 9 | 10 | 11 | 12 | 13 |
| 14 | 15 | 16 | 17 | 18 | 19 | 20 |
| 21 | 22 | 23 | 24 | 25 | 26 | 27 |
| 28 | 29 | 30 | 1 | 2 | 3 | 4 |
| 5 | 6 | 7 | 8 | 9 | 10 | 11 |

# december 2021

| SUN | MON | TUE | WED | THU | FRI | SAT |
|-----|-----|-----|-----|-----|-----|-----|
| 28 | 29 | 30 | 1 | 2 | 3 | 4 |
| 5 | 6 | 7 | 8 | 9 | 10 | 11 |
| 12 | 13 | 14 | 15 | 16 | 17 | 18 |
| 19 | 20 | 21 | 22 | 23 | 24 | 25 |
| 26 | 27 | 28 | 29 | 30 | 31 | 1 |
| 2 | 3 | 4 | 5 | 6 | 7 | 8 |

# MONTH / *year*_____

| SUN | MON | TUE | WED | THU | FRI | SAT |
|-----|-----|-----|-----|-----|-----|-----|
|     |     |     |     |     |     |     |
|     |     |     |     |     |     |     |
|     |     |     |     |     |     |     |
|     |     |     |     |     |     |     |
|     |     |     |     |     |     |     |
|     |     |     |     |     |     |     |

# STAY CONNECTED

## @PUSHPOWERBOSS

**WWW.PUSHPOWERBOSS.COM**

PUSHPOWERBOSS@GMAIL.COM

CPSIA information can be obtained
at www.ICGtesting.com
Printed in the USA
LVHW070012080321
680814LV00003B/149